SUPPLY CHAIN INNOVATION:
Strengthening America's Small Manufacturers

Introduction

U.S. manufacturing is in the midst of a potential resurgence. Since February 2010, manufacturers have added 877,000 jobs – the sector's first sustained job growth since the 1990s.[1] America's 230,000 small manufacturing firms[2] have played a key role in this resurgence, adding the majority of new manufacturing jobs every year, while forming the backbone of U.S. supply chains.

Dense networks of these small manufacturers are vital to the process of taking a product from concept to market, and the exchange of manufacturing know-how across suppliers is essential for the diffusion of the new technologies and innovative processes that give U.S. manufacturing its cutting edge.

However, these networks are under stress. From 2000 to 2010, manufacturing output and investment stagnated as companies offshored production previously done domestically. The U.S. supplier base weakened, raising doubts about the future of manufacturing's contribution to American innovation.[3]

Small manufacturers then and now face steep barriers to innovation – from invention, to commercialization, to the diffusion of new technology. For example, small manufacturers contribute less than one-third of all manufacturing R&D, despite making up 98 percent of manufacturing firms and as a general rule, small firms are one-seventh as likely as large firms to conduct R&D.[4]

As a result, small manufacturers are often in the positon of having to adopt technologies invented by others. Small manufacturers also face unique barriers in accessing the capital and expertise to take on the risk of new technologies. In part because of the challenges they face in adopting new technologies and processes, small manufacturers are only 60 percent as productive as large manufacturers.[5]

Strengthening America's supply chains and the small manufacturers at their core is essential to the long-term competitiveness of U.S. manufacturers both large and small. Manufacturers spend on average 60 percent of the price of their final product on purchased inputs, so differences in the quality and nimbleness of their supply chains can make or break a manufacturer's ability to compete.[6]

Large manufacturers have a critical role to play in cultivating the capabilities of small firms in their supply chains and spurring cross-pollination of expertise across firms. But many currently underinvest in their supply chains because of conflicting internal goals or the fear of strengthening small businesses that may also serve their competitors. By focusing on supplier quality and innovation rather than engaging in a race to the bottom on piece price, companies can send a strong market signal that stimulates innovation by small suppliers, thereby making the entire supply chain more competitive.

The public sector can augment and catalyze private-sector efforts such as those described above. Using its unique innovation assets, the government can help small manufacturers access state-of-the-art research, engineering expertise, and equipment that normally would be out of reach for any one small company. Government can also convene supply chain consortia to develop new technologies, and can highlight best practices in customer-supplier relationships.

For example, the Hollings Manufacturing Extension Partnership at the Department of Commerce is a network of 60 centers and 1,200 manufacturing experts across the country. By providing technical expertise to small manufacturers, the state-federal partnership strengthens the capabilities of individual suppliers and entire supply chains, spurs new linkages between suppliers, and provides small manufacturers with insight into technologies that can revolutionize their business. In addition, the Department of Energy's National Labs, leading national innovation assets, can help small manufacturers access cutting-edge manufacturing equipment, try out technologies and get answers to pressing research challenges through programs like those run by the Los Alamos and Sandia National Laboratories.

The United States has made considerable progress in bolstering American manufacturing since the Great Recession, but there is still more to be done to grow middle-class jobs and help businesses expand in this vital sector. The Administration's focus on reinvesting in the small manufacturers that comprise the core of America's supply chains is just one example of how — through sustained focus and investment across the public and private sectors — the United States can rebuild what was lost and lay a foundation to sustain and deepen the resurgence underway in U.S. manufacturing.

The Increasing Importance of Small Manufacturers and Supply Chains

Dense networks of small- and medium-sized manufacturers increasingly power the engine of America's supply chains. For much of the 20th century, firms were likely to design and build their own products using internally produced parts and proprietary technologies developed by their own employees.[7] In recent decades, such vertical integration has become less common, with many firms focusing instead on a few core

3

competencies and outsourcing other stages of production to suppliers, sometimes thousands of suppliers.

The automobile industry provides just one example. In the 1920s, '30s, and '40s, Ford Motor Company's River Rouge production complex was a mile-and-a-half wide and over a mile long, with 93 buildings and 15.8 million square feet of floor space. In addition to furnaces for making iron and steel, the complex "included a tire-making plant, stamping plant, engine casting plant, frame and assembly plant, transmission plant, radiator plant, tool and die plant, and, at one time, even a paper mill. A massive power plant produced enough electricity to light a city the size of nearby Detroit, and a soybean conversion plant turned soybeans into plastic auto parts." Ford also owned the natural resources needed to produce automobiles: 700,000 acres of forests, iron mines and limestone quarries, coal-rich land, and a rubber plantation. [8]

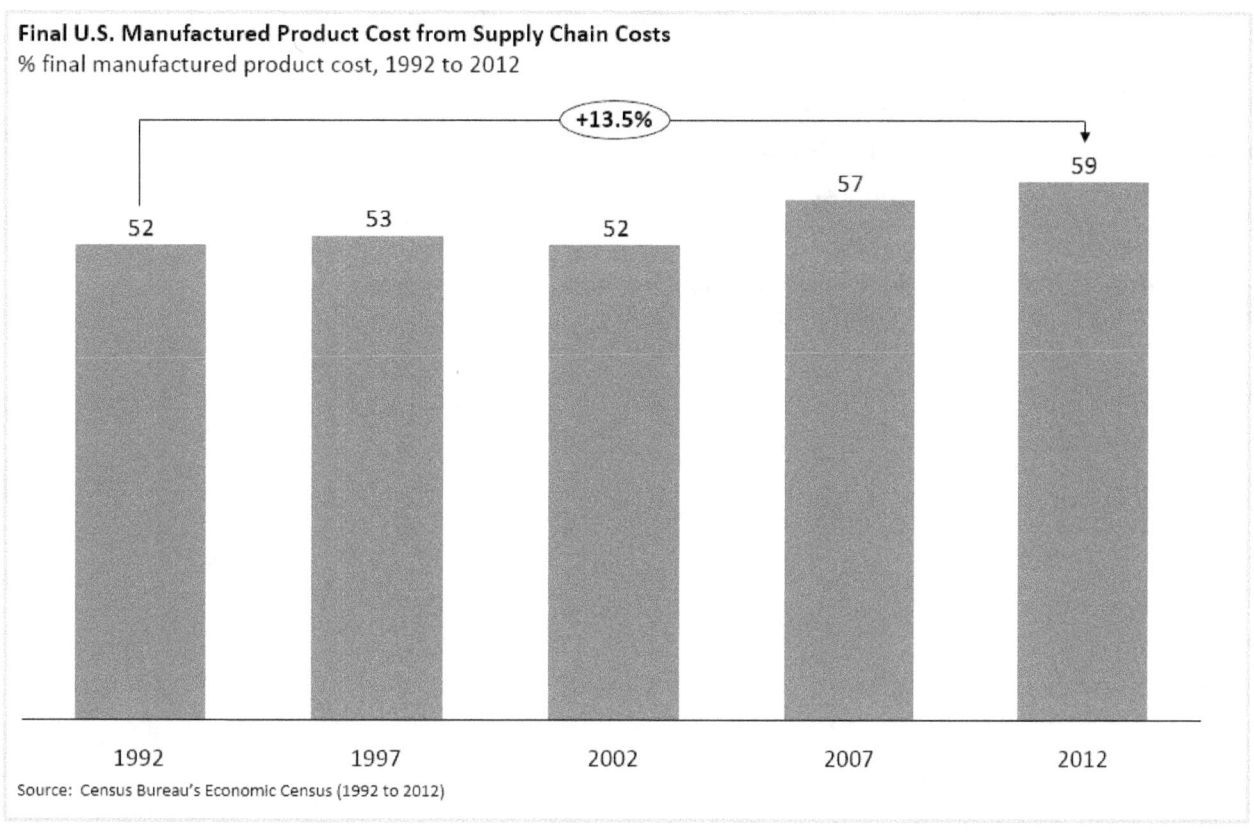

Final U.S. Manufactured Product Cost from Supply Chain Costs
% final manufactured product cost, 1992 to 2012

+13.5%

| 1992 | 1997 | 2002 | 2007 | 2012 |
| 52 | 53 | 52 | 57 | 59 |

Source: Census Bureau's Economic Census (1992 to 2012)

Today, rather than making most of their inputs in company-owned factories or sourcing raw materials from company-owned plantations and mines, most automakers depend on outside firms to design and produce parts. Close to 60 percent of the purchase price of a new car today comes from value added by suppliers, including everything from cup-holders to semiconductors to steering wheels.[9] And the same is true for U.S. manufacturing overall.[10] Far more workers are now employed by suppliers than by the lead firm. For example, Chrysler's Toledo assembly complex employed 2,400 workers in 2011, but even more workers – 3,000 total – were employed in the 200 "Tier 1 suppliers" that shipped parts directly to the Toledo plant. These suppliers included a manufacturer in Dry Ridge, KY that provided the axles, another in Saranac, MI that made the door handles, and yet another factory in Northwood, OH that supplied the seats.[11] Some parts came from foreign countries, such as wiring harnesses from Mexico.

Chrysler's Tier 1 suppliers were, in turn, supplied by Tier 2 suppliers, who themselves were supplied by Tier 3 suppliers, pulling from industries as diverse as computer and electronics manufacturing, textiles, plastic and rubber products, and metal forming. When all the tiers of the supply chain are added up, an automaker may have thousands of suppliers.[12]

As firms shift from in-house production to more distributed production in networks of suppliers, the health of supply chains becomes more important to the competitiveness of both industries and nations. In addition, this shift towards networks of specialized suppliers has raised the importance of small manufacturers to overall growth and employment in manufacturing.

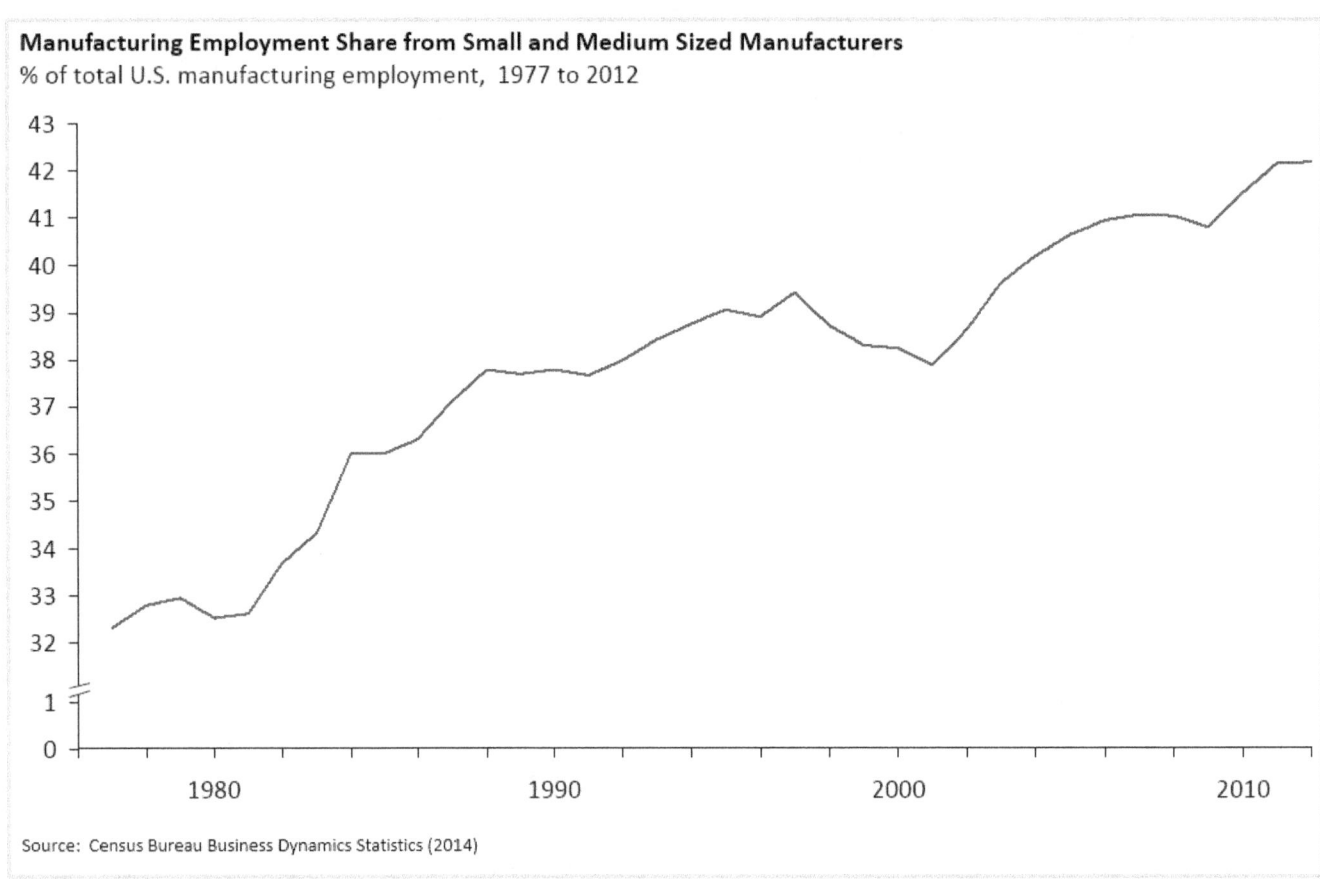

Manufacturing Employment Share from Small and Medium Sized Manufacturers
% of total U.S. manufacturing employment, 1977 to 2012

Source: Census Bureau Business Dynamics Statistics (2014)

Today, more than 230,000 small manufacturers form the backbone of America's supply chains and employ an increasing share of U.S. manufacturing's overall workforce.[13] Throughout the recovery, the majority of new manufacturing jobs have come from small manufacturers (firms with fewer than 500 employees).[14] In the 1980s, small manufacturers accounted for less than a third of all U.S. manufacturing employees. Today, small manufacturers employ 42 percent of all U.S. manufacturing workers, a steady increase of ten percentage points over three decades.[15]

Because small manufacturers play an increasing role in the overall manufacturing sector as members of tightly interdependent supply chains, their ability to keep up with and even lead advances in technology is critical to the competitiveness of U.S. manufacturing overall.

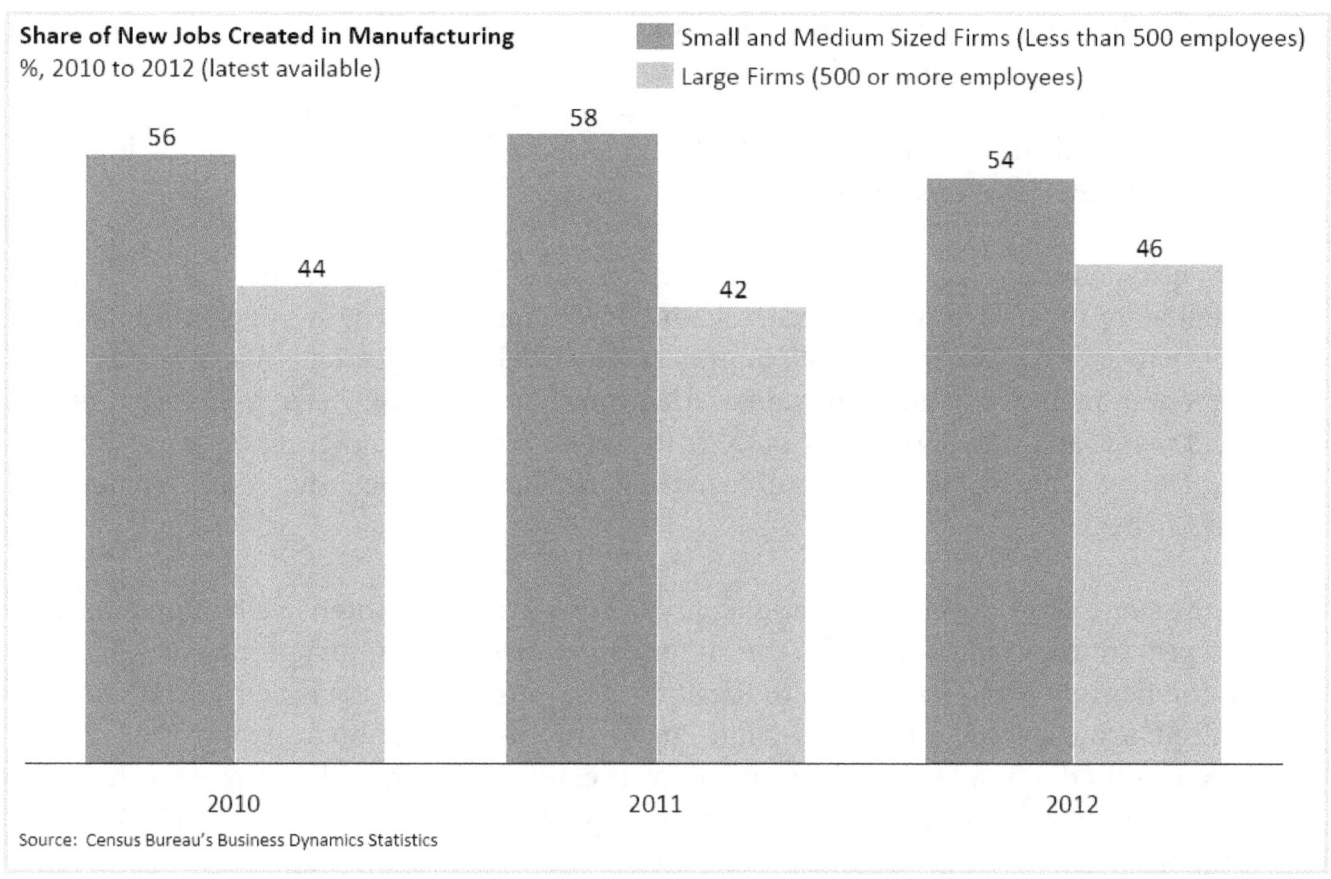

Share of New Jobs Created in Manufacturing
%, 2010 to 2012 (latest available)

Small and Medium Sized Firms (Less than 500 employees)
Large Firms (500 or more employees)

2010: 56 / 44
2011: 58 / 42
2012: 54 / 46

Source: Census Bureau's Business Dynamics Statistics

The Challenge and Reward of Supply Chain Innovation

To stay at the forefront of global production, the U.S. manufacturing sector has stepped up its investment in research and development. U.S. manufacturing R&D, three-quarters of total U.S. private sector R&D, is at an all-time high of nearly $200 billion in 2013.[16] Manufacturers across the United States are investing in cutting-edge processes, advanced materials like carbon fiber and lightweight metals, new sensors and digital controls, and many more new technologies that have the potential to transform U.S. manufacturing.

New technologies such as these contribute to the nation's overall competitiveness only to the extent that they spread throughout U.S. supply chains. Dense networks of small manufacturers in the nation's supply chains are vital to the process of taking a product from concept to market, and the exchange of manufacturing know-how across suppliers is essential for the diffusion of these new technologies that give U.S. manufacturing its cutting edge.[17]

However, small manufacturers face barriers to innovation, with fewer resources, capabilities, internal engineering staff, and financial wherewithal to invest in research and development or to adopt new, potentially risky technologies, no matter how transformative. Economists often delineate three stages in the process of technical change: invention, the first appearance of a new idea; commercialization, the first practical application of the idea; and diffusion, the widespread adoption of the idea. Small suppliers face obstacles in each of these stages.[18]

Invention. Most private-sector R&D is performed by large manufacturers – very few small manufacturers invest in research and development internally which inhibits their ability to invent. Two-thirds of all manufacturing R&D is performed by just the 2 percent of manufacturing companies with more than 500 employees. In fact, 39 percent of all manufacturing R&D is attributable to just 20 large manufacturers, such as Boeing and Dow.[19] Only 2 percent of small firms conduct R&D at all, compared to 14 percent of large firms.[20]

At the same time, the creativity and agility of small, research-intensive manufacturers can be a source of innovation for the larger companies they supply, particularly as large manufacturers look increasingly to R&D partnerships for new ideas and breakthroughs. Indeed, some small manufacturers have made nimble innovation central to their business model. While overall few small firms conduct their own R&D, among those that did, these small businesses had on average 13 percent of their workforce in R&D, compared to only 6 percent at large firms conducting R&D.[21]

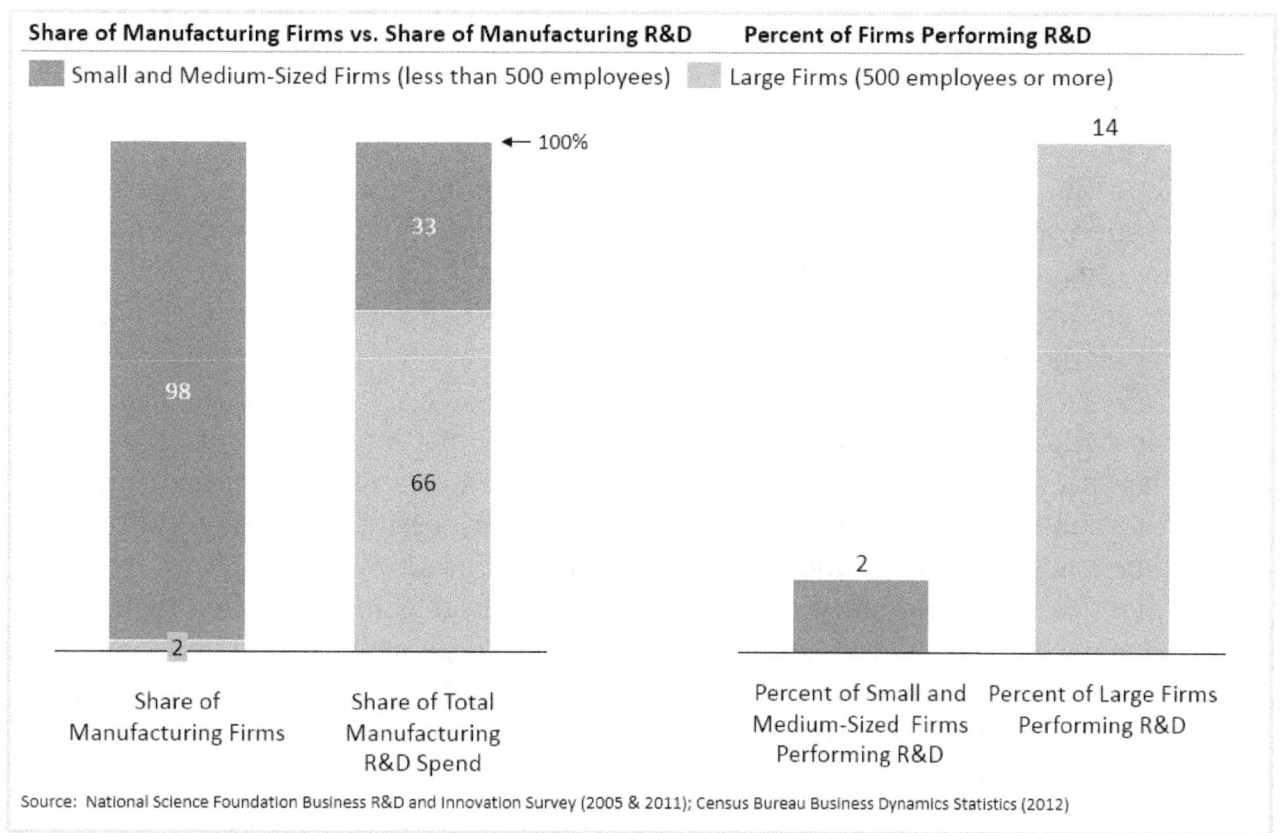

Source: National Science Foundation Business R&D and Innovation Survey (2005 & 2011); Census Bureau Business Dynamics Statistics (2012)

Commercialization. Even when small manufacturers do invest in R&D and this yields an invention, small manufacturers often have trouble finding the capital and connections needed for commercialization.[22] Small manufacturers' lower margins and limited access to capital hampers their investment in new technologies and the extent to which they take risks on technologies that have yet to be widely tested and adopted.[23]

Even with a relatively well-tested technology, upgrading a supplier's tooling and capabilities to meet the needs of a prospective customer can be risky. A supplier has to pay for the new equipment required to start producing a new part but will only get paid when that part is finally being supplied — months and sometimes years later. And if a supplier serves several large manufacturers, the large firms may lack incentive to invest in upgrading the supplier's capabilities if that supplier may also use those capabilities to serve a competitor.

Tighter research and technology linkages between large firms, suppliers, and other small manufacturers in the supply chain can enhance the diffusion of new technologies and lead to productive exchange of knowledge and capabilities. As the fixed cost of prototypes and digital design for smaller firms decreases, the potential for agile small manufacturers to develop new technologies, either on their own or in partnership with larger firms, increases. For example, GE, which re-shored its appliance manufacturing to take innovative products to market more rapidly, is partnering with Local Motors to "crowd source" ideas for new appliances and improvements to existing appliances and to develop prototypes to test these ideas more quickly and efficiently. [24]

Diffusion. Small manufacturers are often slow to adopt new technologies. For example, a recent survey found that less than 60 percent of small manufacturers were experimenting in any way with 3-D printing, a potentially transformative technology that is especially beneficial for small companies due to its flexibility. In contrast, over 75 percent of large firms were using the technology.[25]

Since most R&D is performed by large firms, small manufacturers are usually in the position of needing to adopt a technology that was invented and tested outside their shop. Yet, small manufacturers employ fewer of the engineering and design staff needed to validate a new technology and update processes and products to incorporate it into production. For example, successful adoption of IT-based technology often requires complementary investments in equipment, shop-floor organization, marketing, and training – a scale and scope of expertise that challenges the capabilities of many small firms. [26,27] Small suppliers may also be unaware of new technologies because they lack the resources to track technological developments.[28]

Finally, industry dynamics can hinder investment by small firms. A small firm wishing to adopt new technologies may find it difficult to compete in the near term with rivals intent on competing by cutting corners rather than innovating. While some firms survive based on perennial cost-cutting of this type (such as using lower-quality materials or reducing investment in equipment and training), other small firms in the same industry wishing to invest in innovation can find it difficult to match the prices offered by these competitors. This situation can create a race to the bottom, preventing an entire industry from harnessing technological advances.[29]

In large part because of the significant challenges they face in inventing or adopting new technologies, small manufacturers are significantly less productive than their larger counterparts. Small manufacturing establishments are less than 60 percent as productive as their larger counterparts.[30] Small manufacturers' barriers to innovation ultimately affect all firms in the supply chain. The weaknesses of suppliers accumulate to adversely affect the lead firm, its final products, and its ability to introduce new products to market.

Today, America's small manufacturers, which undergird U.S. supply chains, are once again on the rise. But more needs to be done to rebuild their capabilities and tighten the linkages between firms that can accelerate products to market and spur fruitful cross-pollination of innovation and expertise across firms.

The vitality of the nation's supply chains and the ability of America's small manufacturers to increase their capability with the latest technologies are important to U.S. competitiveness for jobs and investment in manufacturing, broadly. And the strength of its supply chains in many cases determines the ability of an individual manufacturer – even a large firm – to bring products successfully to market. As a result, reinvesting in America's small manufacturers, boosting their technological capabilities, and building tighter linkages between firms should be a public and a private sector priority.

Industry leaders, in particular, have a key role to play in strengthening U.S. supply chains by helping small manufacturers accelerate the adoption of new technologies. Through supplier mentoring and high-road business practices, large firms can expose small manufactures in their supply chains to new technologies while also providing them with greater security to take risks and realize a return on new technologies. In addition, small manufacturers and entire supply chains, by banding together in partnerships focused on technology exploration, can collectively lower the risk of investing in new technologies and coalesce around technology standards that can make collaboration across firms more efficient.

Undertaking these efforts represents a new strategic shift for many large firms which are coming to appreciate the increasing importance of innovative capacity in their supply chains rather than just high-volume, low-cost production. As McKinsey notes, "Many global supply chains are not equipped to cope with the world we are entering. Most were engineered, some brilliantly, to manage stable, high-volume production by capitalizing on labor-arbitrage opportunities available in China and other low-cost countries."[31] Absent a reinvestment in the innovative capacity of their suppliers and tighter linkages and coordination across the supply chain, many large manufacturers may struggle to keep up with the accelerating pace of innovation and consumer demand for rapid product cycles.

Evidence suggests that the following practices help firms promote supplier innovation, especially among small businesses in their supply chains: [32]

1.   Offer suppliers assurance that they will receive a return on investments they make in new technologies and in upgrading their capabilities.

Investments in new capabilities and technologies are inherently risky, especially for small suppliers with tight margins and limited access to capital. Informal assurance from larger partners that these investments are of sufficient value to receive a price premium and continued business can reduce the risk of the investment. And guidance from larger manufacturers about emerging manufacturing technologies, especially those that may require collaborative changes in design between supplier and lead manufacturer, can help suppliers identify those technologies that provide the greatest value.

Bruno Independent Living Aids, a Wisconsin maker of accessibility solutions such as stair lifts, was able to convince a key supplier to make an investment in technology to solve its production needs through informal assurances. A few years ago, Bruno needed to find a way to inhibit rust on products used in outdoor environments. Bruno's painting supplier, Ad-Tech Industries, invested in a new "E-coat" paint process that allows paint to adhere to metal very tightly using an electrostatic charge, thus reducing rust. The equipment cost over one million dollars, a large investment for a small supplier.

However, because Bruno was willing to make an informal assurance that it would buy capacity on the new machine at a reasonable price, Ad-Tech's risk in making the investment fell significantly. As a result, Bruno has a solution to its quality problem, and Ad-Tech has a new capability that benefits other customers as well, thus strengthening the whole manufacturing ecosystem.[33]

Similarly, Atlantic Tool and Die in Strongsville, Ohio had a single small factory when it began supplying small stamped parts to Honda in 1988. Today, Atlantic Tool and Die credits its partnership with Honda for enabling it to grow to six plants in the United States and abroad. In particular, Honda's technical assistance on new technologies and commitment to future business enabled Atlantic Tool and Die to invest in robotic welding that made it attractive to new customers while benefiting Honda through improved quality and economies of scale. The skill that Atlantic gained enabled the firm to invest, early on, in putting sensors in its dies, a technology that reduced stamping errors by more than 90 percent.[34]

2. Promote information-sharing and make changes in their own operations as a result of supplier suggestions.

Communication with suppliers may reveal actions by lead firms that turn out to be costly for suppliers – costs that ultimately may be passed on to the buying firm. For example, large companies often undertake policies such as frequent schedule changes or late payments that impose far greater costs on their suppliers than they realize. Other firms may allow suppliers to speak only to purchasing agents, in an attempt to preserve their bargaining power. However, blocking communication with engineers may mean that they miss out on suppliers' best ideas and joint problem-solving that would benefit both firms.

An example from Itron, a maker of gas and electric meters, shows the value of joint problem-solving. A new Itron product had a terminal in which the contact area was coated with silver and cadmium, both very expensive metals. Combining their expertise, Itron and the supplier were able to reduce the area needed for contact, saving over a third of the cost of the component. Itron's practice of frequent communication and joint problem-solving with its suppliers is a growing competitive strength for the company. [35] These benefits of coordination among firms are magnified in the case of a breakthrough technology, such as a new material that requires a different production or joining process.

3.   Use a "Total Cost of Ownership" approach in making purchasing decisions.

Innovation is greatly facilitated if lead firms choose suppliers not on the narrow basis of low piece prices, but instead use a "Total Cost of Ownership" (TCO) approach, which considers the many kinds of costs to the buyer associated with the acquisition, transportation, and storage of products within the supply chain.[36] These costs include shipping costs, shipping time, storage costs and risk of damage or obsolescence of inventory, quality costs, travel costs for supplier oversight, currency fluctuations, intellectual property risk, financing costs, and risk of interruptions to the supply chain.[37]

Consideration of this broader set of costs encourages suppliers to innovate to find new ways to maximize value for the supply chain as a whole. For example, a supplier of advanced fuel systems was pursuing a large multi-year contract with one of the Detroit automakers. The automaker's purchasing department demanded a price reduction, noting that a competing supplier had submitted a bid at a significantly lower price per piece. The first supplier's patented catalyst technology used a wash coat technique to place precisely the precious metals used in its system, resulting in reduced use of the metals, lower cost of operation, and more effective oxidation of hydrocarbons and carbon monoxide. After the supplier's marketing team quantified and documented the improvements they offered, the automaker agreed to pay a premium compared to the lower-priced bidder. Even with the premium, the automaker's costs were lower than with the competing supplier because of the advanced technology.[38]

Research shows that practices such as those adopted by Itron, Bruno Independent Living Aids, and Honda – of involving suppliers early in product design, providing technical assistance, engaging in frequent communication, and being willing to share costs – are highly correlated with supplier willingness to invest in new technology.[39]

Unfortunately, these beneficial technology collaborations and efforts by larger companies to help supply chains upgrade their capabilities are too infrequent.[40] In some cases, large manufacturers will underinvest in their suppliers fearing that improvements in suppliers' capabilities might also serve their competitors.

Supply Chain Innovation in the Automobile Industry

Introducing breakthrough technologies benefits greatly from coordination among firms, including suppliers that can improvise, do new things, and understand the whole as full partners in innovation. One example is increasing the energy efficiency of cars by using lightweight materials: a ten percent reduction in a vehicle's weight can lead to a six to eight percent reduction in fuel use. To introduce new, sophisticated light-weight metals into the production process requires combining the expertise of large automakers and their suppliers.

For example, "dual-phase" steel becomes strong only if it is stretched, so a lighter-weight part will fail unless ridges are included in the design to ensure that all areas of the part are stretched as it is stamped. In contrast to traditional steel, whose properties are well understood, designing the nature of the ridges required is still more of an art, and requires communication between the small tool and die shops, which have the knowledge of what kinds of ridges are needed, and the large automakers who want to use the new materials in their cars.

Here, industry learning overall can be accelerated by encouraging greater collaboration among automakers and their suppliers, and adopting supplier contracts that allow for experimentation by recognizing the reality of occasional failures. One example of collaboration is underway at the Center for Automotive Research (CAR) in Ann Arbor, Michigan. CAR leads the Coalition for Automotive Lightweighting Materials (CALM)—a consortium of 30 suppliers and small manufacturers that work together with automakers to identify barriers to the introduction of lightweight materials, and develop solutions enabling their use.

In other cases, a near-term focus on getting the lowest price for a particular component in the supply chain may obscure the long-term productivity benefits of encouraging a supplier's investments in new technologies, or preserving a supplier's margins for reinvestment in new capabilities.[41] And forming and sustaining cross-industry technology collaborations between small businesses is not easy – especially when many small manufacturers lack sufficient engineering and research personnel to easily participate in these collaborations.

The public sector can build on private-sector efforts such as those described above, acting as a catalyst for technology acceleration to benefit the supply chain as a whole. Government can help small manufacturers update their technology, processes, and capabilities, and help small manufacturers access state of the art research and equipment that normally would be out of reach for any one small company. The public sector can also play a catalytic role, by convening supply chain consortia to develop new technologies, and highlight best practices in customer-supplier relationships.

Promising initiatives along these lines are already underway:[42]

The Hollings Manufacturing Extension Partnership (MEP), created in 1988 and part of the Commerce Department's National Institute of Standards and Technology (NIST), was designed to overcome some of these challenges by providing small businesses access to management and technological expertise in 60 centers across the country. Every day, its more than 1,200 experts consult with manufacturers to help them improve their processes and identify opportunities to adopt new technologies or take new products to market. Today, over 30,000 manufacturers benefit from this expertise and network.

Recognizing the growing importance of supply chains and realizing that stronger connections between firms can help small manufacturers upgrade their capabilities, the Manufacturing Extension Partnership is expanding the successful supply chain and technology acceleration services for small manufacturers piloted over the last few years. These services include:

- *Supplier Improvement and Supply Chain Optimization* – MEP's Supplier Improvement program helps individual small manufacturers identify process improvements and technology upgrades to help them better compete within supply chains. And working across an entire supply chain, MEP's Supply Chain Optimization Program helps manufacturers build dynamic supply chains by assessing total cost of ownership, building deeper supplier communication, and helping suppliers upgrade their quality.[43]

- *Supplier Scouting and Business-to-Business Networks* – These programs help manufacturers find a U.S. supplier either through MEP's network of 30,000 manufacturers across the country or through new regional business-to-business network projects and manufacturing exchanges that directly link buyers to suppliers who have the right capabilities.

- *Supply Chain Technology Acceleration* – MEP helps small manufacturers within specific supply chains identify technologies, acquire technology-driven market intelligence, and mitigate potential risk of new technologies by modeling their application to small manufacturers' existing processes.

In addition, federal agencies such as the Departments of Defense and Energy have begun to partner with firms of all sizes to strengthen supply chains in manufacturing industries important to their missions.

The Department of Defense Office of Economic Adjustment (OEA) supports state and local governments in responding to changes in defense programs that affect communities, including base closures or expansions, and incompatibilities between military operations and local development.[44] OEA's Defense Industry Adjustment (DIA) program works with supply chains, seeking to help its customers improve their resiliency in their respective defense industrial bases. While DIA works to help dislocated workers and impacted firms adjust to demand shocks from changes in defense spending, another major component of the DIA program is helping communities understand the economic clusters that comprise their local, regional, or state defense industrial base. In addition, DIA helps these communities understand how their industrial base interacts with other states or regions.

One recent DIA project is the Virginia DoD Procurement Economic Impact Evaluation Model.[45] The model is a supply-chain mapping of DoD contract awards, including sales and employment impacts, available for public use. It provides state-, county-, and local-level details about current and projected economic impacts of DoD contract spending. Similar projects are underway in Colorado, southern California, and New Jersey.

The Department of Energy (DoE) maintains 17 national labs in the United States. The labs engage in basic and applied technology R&D and provide a forum for the exchange of technology and ideas between regional firms, universities, and economic development intermediaries.[46] The New Mexico Small Business Assistance (NMSBA) program helps small businesses in the area by providing access to experts at the local Los Alamos National Laboratory and Sandia National Laboratories.[47] Technical assistance is funded by the state and provided to businesses free-of-charge, but access is competitive. To help small businesses compete for funding, the NMSBA created a national lab voucher program that since 2000 has helped over 1,000 small businesses gain access to the Los Alamos and Sandia labs. The state government provides the funding for the vouchers through a partnership with the NMSBA.

Ten projects developed by small businesses in New Mexico leveraging technical expertise and assistance provided by the Los Alamos and Sandia labs were recognized in 2012 for their innovation.[48] Technologies of Santa Fe, a small manufacturer, worked with the labs to develop a solar thermal ice-making product to deliver life-saving vaccines throughout the world in storage containers that use solar energy to maintain low temperatures.

The SupplierPay Initiative, a partnership between the federal government and the private sector, has resulted in nearly 50 companies signing a pledge to improve payment terms to their suppliers.[49] Because small suppliers are often subject to more stringent credit restraints than larger companies, they have difficulty securing working capital when buyers lengthen payment terms. This, in turn, passes costs back onto the buyers in the form of higher piece prices or reduced innovation. Faster payment terms free up working capital for small suppliers to use for investments in worker training orinnovation.[50] Many of these companies also play a prominent role in the American Supplier Initiative, often participating as corporate buyers in a series of nationwide events designed to engage small business suppliers in corporate supply chains.

Restoring the vitality of America's supply chains and the small manufacturers at their core is essential to the long-term competitiveness of U.S. manufacturing. The Administration's focus on reinvesting in America's supply chains is just one example of how joint public-private sector efforts can strengthen the foundation of these key elements of the U.S. economy.

Now is the time for additional action to build on these efforts and strengthen our manufacturing base. As discussed above, market-based incentives by themselves are inadequate to ensure sufficient investment in supply chains. There are ample opportunities for government at all levels to partner with the private sector to promote supply chain innovation and thus foster a continued manufacturing renaissance, both now and into the future.

Appendix: An International Perspective

Governments around the world recognize the importance of fostering innovation throughout the supply chain. Below are examples of these efforts from around the globe.

Germany

German firms have a diverse set of resources at their disposal. Both the firms and the government contribute to the development and maintenance of these relationships.[51] Firms invest heavily in the capabilities of their workers, many of whom also participate in apprenticeship programs sponsored by the government. When firms consider bringing a new idea to market, they often rely on collaboration with their suppliers to develop new technologies and work through the initial phases of scale-up together.[52]

The industrial ecosystem in Germany involves many players – lead firms and suppliers, trade associations, unions, industrial collective research consortia, industrial research centers and associations, Fraunhofer Institutes, university-industry collaboratives, technical advisory committees, and others – who all work together to create an environment that supports innovation.[53] These collaborations are numerous and are not a new phenomenon—a survey of 744 industrial collective research projects in German between 2003 and 2005 identified almost 300 organizations involved in these projects.[54] The German government provides some limited funding through these organizations, but the convening power of government is one of the greatest benefits to all firms from these arrangements.[55] The government funding is used to incentivize collaborations; for example, the government provided 40 million Euros (matched by private industry) to the photovoltaic cluster Solarvalley Mitteldeutschland to match the same funding from industry for a five-year project on grid parity that brought together firms, universities, and research institutes.[56] They also provide innovation vouchers to firms to help catalyze innovation and connect them with researchers at universities or other firms.[57]

United Kingdom

In the United Kingdom, the Manufacturing Advisory Service (MAS), through nine regional centers, provides multiple supports to SMEs. Services include a helpline providing technical assistance, consulting services on process improvement, and networking and training events including best-practices factory visits.[58] These services complement existing supplier mentorship programs provided by lead firms.[59]

The UK has also created a Technology Strategy Board (TSB) with a goal of increasing supply chain R&D collaboration. The TSB also facilitates supply chain partnership opportunities through its Collaborative R&D calls and Feasibility Studies where companies can test new ideas and get customer feedback. Many of these collaborations take place at seven High Value Manufacturing Catapult (HVM Catapult) centers. HVM Catapult provides companies and suppliers open-access equipment and technical assistance. An example of a technological innovation that came out of a HVM Catapult center was the MEGA-FLUTE tooling technology, which has the potential to revolutionize milling cutter technology in the aerospace industry, leading to significant reductions in cost and capital expenditures.[60]

Canada[61]

Canada's Industrial Research Assistance Program (IRAP) helps SMEs build their innovation and new product development capacity by providing technology assistance through a network of 220 Industrial Technology Advisors (ITAs) located in 90 communities throughout Canada.[62] The ITAs connect SMEs with Canadian universities and national laboratories so that the institutions can share emerging technologies and knowledge. IRAP also directly funds R&D and innovation at SMEs.

As in Germany, the Canadian government provides innovation vouchers to firms and provides financial support to SMEs to hire recent college graduates. In some cases, the newly-minted employees with technical degrees are partially supervised by IRAP personnel. A key issue in having small firms use the innovation vouchers is defining an appropriate problem – one which can be solved by the labs and whose solution is also beneficial to firms. The hands-on involvement by experienced IRAP personnel, plus the proximity to the operation of the recent graduate, helps firms to define a problem for which they could productively use an innovation voucher or other program.

Productivity Alberta, started by the government of Alberta in 2008, has assigned MBA students to SMEs to identify and help solve innovation, technical, and scientific challenges by leveraging resources at their graduate schools.[63]

[1] Economics and Statistics Administration analysis using data from the Bureau of Labor Statistics' Current Employment Statistics (CES). CES data may be accessed online at: http://www.bls.gov/ces/.

[2] Economics and Statistics Administration analysis using data from the Census Bureau's Business Dynamics Statistics (BDS). BDS data may be accessed online at: http://www.census.gov/ces/dataproducts/bds/.

[3] See Berger, Suzanne, *Making in America: From Innovation to Market*, MIT Task Force on Production in the Innovation Economy, The MIT Press, 2013; Gary P. Pisano and Willy C. Shih, *Producing Prosperity: Why America Needs a Manufacturing Renaissance*, Harvard Business Review Press, 2012.

[4] Economics and Statistics Administration analysis using data from the National Science Foundation's 2011 Business R&D and Innovation Survey (BRDIS) and the Census Bureau's 2011 Statistics of U.S. Businesses (SUSB). BRDIS data may be accessed online at: http://www.nsf.gov/statistics/srvyindustry/about/brdis/. SUSB data may be accessed online at: http://www.census.gov/econ/susb/.

[5] National Institute of Standards and Technology analysis using data from the Census Bureau's 2007 Economic Census. Economic Census data may be accessed online at: http://www.census.gov/econ/census/.

[6] Economics and Statistics Administration analysis using data from the Census Bureau's 2012 Economic Census. For this calculation, purchased inputs includes: materials, services and expenses, contract work, and energy.

[7] Dedrick, Jason, Kenneth L. Kraemer, and Greg Linden, "Who Profits from Innovation in Global Value Chains? A Study of the iPod and notebook PCs," Personal Computing Industry Center, UC Irvine, May 2008, available at: http://web.mit.edu/is08/pdf/Dedrick_Kraemer_Linden.pdf (last accessed March 2015); A.D. Chandler Jr., *The Visible Hand: The Managerial Revolution in American Business*, Harvard University Press, 1977.

[8] See The Henry Ford webpage, History of the River Rouge, available at: - http://www.thehenryford.org/rouge/historyofrouge.aspx (last accessed January 2015).

[9] Klier, Thomas and James Rubenstein, *Who Really Made your car?: Restructuring and Geographic Change in the Auto Industry*, Upjohn Press, 2008.

[10] U.S. Census Bureau's Economic Census, 2012

[11] The White House, "The Resurgence of the American Automotive Industry," Office of the Press Secretary, June 2011, available at: http://www.whitehouse.gov/sites/default/files/uploads/auto_report_06_01_11.pdf (last accessed January 2015).

[12] Ibid.

[13] Economics and Statistics Administration analysis using data from the Census Bureau's Business Dynamics Statistics (BDS).

[14] Economics and Statistics Administration analysis using data from the Census Bureau's Business Dynamics Statistics (BDS). BDS shows that from 1980 to 2012, 52 percent of new manufacturing jobs were created by firms

with fewer than 500 employees. During that time, only 46 percent of the job losses were from these firms, so they contributed positively to job creation over this time.

[15] Ibid.

[16] Dollar values are inflation-adjusted. Data from Bureau of Economic Analysis, Table 5.6.6. Available at: http://www.bea.gov/iTable/iTable.cfm?reqid=9&step=3&isuri=1&903=332#reqid=9&step=3&isuri=1&903=332.

[17] Berger, Suzanne, *Making in America: From Innovation to Market*, MIT Task Force on Production in the Innovation Economy, The MIT Press, 2013; Gary P. Pisano and Willy C. Shih, *Producing Prosperity: Why America Needs a Manufacturing Renaissance*, Harvard Business Review Press, 2012.

[18] One might argue that a lack of innovation by small firms is not problematic, i.e., that it makes sense for lead firms to specialize in innovation, while suppliers focus on production. However, increasing evidence suggests that this division of labor may be suboptimal. First, there are significant spillovers from production to product innovation; when product engineers are not near the production site, there may be fewer product innovations. Second, lack of process knowledge means that suppliers are less likely to generate or adopt innovative processes. See Pisano and Shih.

[19] Economics and Statistics Administration analysis using data from National Science Foundation's 2005 Business R&D and Innovation Survey.

[20] Economics and Statistics Administration analysis using data from the National Science Foundation's 2011 Business R&D and Innovation Survey and the Census Bureau's 2011 SUSB.

[21] Economics and Statistics Administration analysis using data from the Census Bureau's 2011 BRDIS.

[22] Advanced Manufacturing Partnership report, "Accelerating U.S. Advanced Manufacturing," President's Council of Advisors on Science and Technology, Executive Office of the President, October 2014, available at: http://www.whitehouse.gov/sites/default/files/microsites/ostp/PCAST/amp20_report_final.pdf (last accessed March 2015).

[23] See Helper, Nicholson, and Noonan. "The Economic Benefits of Reducing Supplier Working Capital Costs," available at: http://www.esa.doc.gov/sites/default/files/supplierpayv25.pdf (last accessed March 2015).

[24] Gabrielle Karol, "Local Motors Bringing Crowdsourced Innovation to GE," Fox Business, March 18, 2014, available at http://smallbusiness.foxbusiness.com/technology-web/2014/03/18/local-motors-bringing-crowdsourced-innovation-to-ge/.

[25] PWC, "3D printing and the new shape of industrial manufacturing," June 2014, available at: https://www.pwc.se/sv_SE/se/verkstad/assets/3d-printing-and-the-new-shape-of-industrial-manufacturing.pdf (last accessed March 2015).

[26] Kelley, Maryellen and Susan Helper, "Firm Size and Capabilities, Regional Agglomeration, and the Adoption of New Technology," Economics of Innovation and New Technology, Vol. 8, Issue 1-2, 1999, available at: http://www.tandfonline.com/doi/abs/10.1080/10438599900000005?journalCode=gein20#.VP3w9_zF98E (last accessed March 2015); Daniel D. Luria, "Why Markets Tolerate Mediocre Manufacturing," *Challenge*, July-August 1996, available at: http://business.highbeam.com/137644/article-1G1-18544973/why-markets-tolerate-mediocre-manufacturing (last accessed March 2015).

[27] Brynjolfsson, Erik and Lorin M. Hitt, "Computing Productivity: Firm-Level Evidence," MIT Sloan Working Paper No. 4210-01, June 2003, available at: http://papers.ssrn.com/sol3/papers.cfm?abstract_id=290325 (last accessed March 2015); Bartel, Ann, Casey Ichniowski, and Kathryn Shaw, "How Does Information Technology Affect Productivity? Plant-Level Comparisons of Product Innovation, Process Improvement, and Worker Skills," Quarterly Journal of Economics, November 2007, available at: http://www.ppge.ufrgs.br/GIACOMO/arquivos/ecop137/bartel-ichniowski-shaw-2007.pdf (last accessed March 2015).

[28] Ibid.

[29] Daron Acemoglu, "Good Jobs versus Bad Jobs," *Journal of Labor Economics* 19 (2001), 1-21; Michael Porter, Competitive Advantage: Creating and Sustaining Superior Performance. New York: Simon and Schuster, 1980.

[30] National Institute of Standards and Technology analysis using data from the Census Bureau's 2007 Economic Census. This productivity differential is not explained by large and small firms competing in different industries; these productivity differences persist even when controlling for narrow industries. In fact, industry effects explain only about 10 percent of productivity differentials. Within 4-digit NAICS codes, the most productive firms are, on average, three times as productive as the least productive firms. One determinant of these intra-industry

differentials is firm size. See Syverson, Chad, "The Importance of Measuring Dispersion in Firm-Level Outcomes," *IZA World of Labor*, May 2014, available at: http://home.uchicago.edu/syverson/SyversonWoL.pdf (last accessed January 2015).

[31] Malik, Yogesh; Alex Niemeyer; and Brian Ruwadi, "Building the supply chain of the future," McKinsey & Company, *McKinsey Quarterly*, January 2011, available at: http://www.mckinsey.com/insights/operations/building_the_supply_chain_of_the_future.

[32] A vast literature describes the potential benefits to lead firms of collaborative relations with suppliers. A review article finds significant benefits to trusting relationships in terms of reduced cost, defect rates, lead times, and increases in investment, responsiveness, and problem-solving behavior. Delbufalo, Emanuela, "Outcomes of inter-organizational trust in supply chain relationships: a systematic literature review and a meta-analysis of the empirical evidence", Supply Chain Management: An International Journal, Vol. 17 Issue 4 –2012, available at: http://dx.doi.org/10.1108/13598541211246549 (last accessed March 2015). Extensive study suggests that a key part of the success of firms such as Toyota and Honda was due to their investments in such relationships with their suppliers. Gibbons, Robert and Rebecca Henderson, "Relational Contracts and Organizational Capabilities," *Organization Science*, Volume 23, Issue 5, September-October 2012 Note that being a Toyota supplier was not "a cozy relationship," as one manager of a supplier company pointed out (see Susan Helper and Rebecca Henderson, "Management Practices, Relational Contracts, and the Decline of General Motors," Journal of Economic Perspectives, Vol. 28, No. 1, Winter 2014, available at: https://www.aeaweb.org/articles.php?doi=10.1257/jep.28.1.49). Toyota pushed its suppliers very hard to reduce costs and avoid defects; it reduced the market share of suppliers who did not meet these strict goals; and it exited the relationship completely if improvement was not forthcoming.

[33] Bruno Independent Living Aids, interview and plant visit), Oconomowoc, WI, February 27, 2015.

[34] Stevens, Merieke, John Paul MacDuffie, Susan Helper, "Reorienting and recalibrating inter-organizational relationships: Strategies for achieving optimal trust," *Organization Studies*, forthcoming.

[35] Itron, interview and plant visit, West Union, SC, February 24, 2015

[36] NIST MEP, "U.S. Supply Chains: Insights into the Challenges and a Foundational Roadmap toward Global Competitiveness," U.S. Department of Commerce, available at: http://mepsupplychain.org/wp-content/uploads/2013/08/SupplyChain_Whitepaper.pdf (March 2015).

[37] See Department of Commerce's Assess Costs Everywhere (ACE) tool at: http://acetool.commerce.gov/ and Terry Weiner, "The Importance of Total Cost of Ownership (TCO)," CMTC Manufacturing Blog, January 21, 2014, available at: http://www.cmtc.com/blog/bid/156131/The-Importance-of-Total-Cost-of-Ownership-TCO (last accessed January 2015).

[38] Kotler Marketing Group, private communication, March 5, 2015.

[39] Zhang, Chun, John W. Henke Jr., and Sridhar Viswanathan, "Reciprocity between buyer cost sharing and supplier technology sharing," *Journal of Operations Management*, 27, 2009, available at: http://www.ppi1.com/wp-content/uploads/2012/09/JOM-Supplier-Innovation-Nov-Dec-2009.pdf (last accessed March 2015.)

[40] For example, the technique used by Itron in the example above, called "value analysis/value engineering" is not widely adopted in the US despite strong evidence of its effectiveness. A 2011 survey of auto suppliers found that less than one-third had adopted the technique. Jenny Kuan and Susan Helper, "What Goes on Under the Hood? How Engineers Innovate in the Automotive Supply Chain," in Engineering in a Global Economy, Richard Freeman and Hal Salzman, eds, NBER, forthcoming.

[41] For evidence of "short-termism" generally, see "Report of the Commission on Inclusive Prosperity," Center for American Progress, January 2015, available at: https://cdn.americanprogress.org/wp-content/uploads/2015/01/IPC-PDF-full.pdf (last accessed March 2015).

[42] The appendix provides examples of programs in other nations that may be instructive for the U.S.

[43] These new services build on Accelerate, a Wisconsin Manufacturing Extension Partnership (WMEP) program that is used by over 400 suppliers across many different industries. The goal of Accelerate is to assist manufacturers to reduce their Manufacturing Critical-path Time (MCT). MCT is defined as the time between when a customer places an order to receipt of the first piece of that order. Reducing lead times is important because longer lead times cause firms to hold more inventory, often adding 20-30 percent to product costs. The U.S. Defense Logistics Agency recently reviewed 195 Department of Defense suppliers that had received training, and found that each company saw an average reduction in inventory of $132,000, as well as a $98,000 reduction in internal quality-

related waste, and a $75,000 reduction in other direct operational costs. In addition, these suppliers experienced improvements in their on-time deliveries and their quality, as measured by their customers. Orders saw quicker turnaround, and MCT was cut by 50 percent.

[44] For more information, see the OEA's website, available at: http://www.oea.gov/about/oea.

[45] For more information, see: http://www.chmuraecon.com/blog/2014/may/virginia-department-of-defense-dod-procurement-economic-impact-evaluation-model/.

[46] Andes, Scott, Mark Muro, and Matthew Stepp, "Going Local: Connecting the National Labs to their Regions for Innovation and Growth," Brookings, "The information Technology & Innovation Foundation, and the Center for Clean Energy Innovation," September 2014, available at: http://www.brookings.edu/~/media/Research/Files/Reports/2014/09/10-national-labs/BMPP_DOE_Brief.pdf?la=en (last accessed March 2015).

[47] New Mexico Small Business Administration brochure, available online at: http://www.nmsbaprogram.org/userfiles/2014_NMSBA_ProspectBro_January_2015_FNL.pdf.

[48] "Los Alamos, Sandia National Laboratories recognize New Mexico small businesses for innovation," New Mexico Small Business Administration, May 1, 2012, available at: http://www.nmsbaprogram.org/news/detail/22 (last accessed March 2015).

[49] The White House, Office of the Press Secretary, "FACT SHEET: President Obama's SupplierPay Initiative Expands; 21 Additional Companies Pledge to Strengthen America's Small Businesses," November 17, 2014, available at: http://www.whitehouse.gov/the-press-office/2014/11/17/fact-sheet-president-obama-s-supplierpay-initiative-expands-21-additiona (last accessed March 2015).

[50] See Helper, Nicholson, and Noonan. "The Economic Benefits of Reducing Supplier Working Capital Costs," available at: http://www.esa.doc.gov/sites/default/files/supplierpayv25.pdf (last accessed March 2015).

[51] Berger. Also, several German states co-finance the placement of recent Ph.D. graduates with SME manufacturers. In Brandenburg state's program, the state covers 50 percent of the cost for an SME to employ a recent Ph.D. graduate for up to two years according to in person interviews conducted by Stephen Ezell and Robert D. Atkinson. See "International Benchmarking of Countries' Policies and Programs Supporting SME Manufacturers," Information Technology and Innovation Foundation, September 14, 2011, available at: http://www.itif.org/publications/international-benchmarking-countries-policies-and-programs-supporting-sme-manufacturers (last accessed March 2015).

[52] Berger.

[53] Fraunhofer is Europe's largest application-oriented research organization. Its 66 institutes and research units are located throughout Germany. See more at: http://www.fraunhofer.de/en/about-fraunhofer.html.

[54] Berger.

[55] Ibid.

[56] Ibid.

[57] Ezell and Atkinson.

[58] Ibid.

[59] United Kingdom Department for Business and Innovation Skills, Strengthening UK Supply Chains, January 2014, available at: http://www.mbsportal.bl.uk/taster/subjareas/techinnov/bis/15994914_515_strengthening_supply.pdf.

[60] Ibid.

[61] Ezell and Atkinson.

[62] See also the National Research Council of Canada, "IRAP: Mandate, Mission, Values, Program Goals and Strategic Objectives," available at: http://www.nrc-cnrc.gc.ca/eng/irap/index.html.

[63] Ezell and Atkinson interview with Lori Schmidt, Senior Director, Productivity Alberta, July 6, 2011 as cited in footnote 58. In 2011, Productivity Alberta became Go Productivity, a private non-profit that helps Canadian companies identify and address gaps in productivity, maximize resources, and be more efficient. For more information see the Go Productivity website at: http://goproductivity.ca/.